IRRATIONAL FAITH

BREAKTHROUGH TO THE BLESSING

BY
ANTHONY L. TAYLOR

Copyright © 2014 by Anthony L. Taylor

Irrational Faith
Breakthrough to the Blessing
by Anthony L. Taylor

Printed in the United States of America

ISBN 9781629524450

All rights reserved solely by the author. The author guarantees all contents are original and do not infringe upon the legal rights of any other person or work. No part of this book may be reproduced in any form without the permission of the author. The views expressed in this book are not necessarily those of the publisher.

Unless otherwise indicated, Bible quotations are taken from the New International Version (NIV). Copyright © 1973, 1978, 1984, 2011 by Biblica, Inc.™. Used by permission. All rights reserved.

www.xulonpress.com

Table of Contents

Dedication vii
Acknowledgments ix
Introduction xi

Chapter One: Be Converted 13
Chapter Two: Be Sure 25
Chapter Three: Be Prayerful 39
Chapter Four: Be Persistent 55
Chapter Five: Be Mobile 67

Conclusion 79

Dedication

I dedicate this book to my best friend, irrational faith partner and love of my life, Paula Jean. You have pushed me to the highest mountain peaks, walked with me through the deepest valleys and provided encouraging words on discouraging days. I am truly blessed by your love.

ACKNOWLEDGMENTS

I would like to thank my entire family for their faith and confidence in me.

To my sons Lee and Drew, who sacrificed time with Dad so that I could fulfill the call of God. You give me purpose!

To my daughter Christie, I reserve a special place for you in my heart.

A very special thank-you to my mom and dad for your love, support and continued encouragement to dream big.

A personal thanks to my sisters for the admiration and love you've given.

I owe a debt of gratitude to my mother-in-law and father-in-law for continued prayers and support.

To the leaders and members of my home church, St. Mark United Church of Christ; thanks for developing my faith in the early years.

To the people of God who attended military chapels weekly to listen to the message of Jesus; thanks for allowing me to be your pastor for the past fourteen years.

A special thanks to my friends and professional colleagues, Mrs. Cho and Mrs. Choi, for your dedication and support during my time as director of the Family Life Center in Yongsan, Korea. Go Dream Team!

Finally, I am sincerely grateful to the most high God for the idea, guidance, wisdom and inspiration through our Lord and Savior, Jesus Christ, and the Holy Spirit throughout this entire process.

INTRODUCTION

Irrational faith is not a call to take action in the absence of rational thinking or logic. Rather, it is the belief that only God can do all things. It is trusting God's magnificent power in the face of extreme circumstances. We are rational beings with the highest intelligence, but irrational faith takes us outside of the realm of human possibilities. Rational thinking sets limits, but irrational faith focuses on God in unsolvable circumstances. Irrational faith is completely abandoning the belief that our bankrolls, abilities and intellect are our only means of security. Our resources and attitudes alone cannot define our faith; faith must be developed by obeying God's word through the storms of life. During these times, we rely on God's provisions, promises and overall concern for us, revealed in the Word. The Israelites at the Red Sea had accepted the fate of impending death, but God parted the waters, and they were able to safely cross on dry land (see Exodus 14:1-30). In a crowd of more than 5,000 hungry people, Jesus miraculously multiplied five barley loaves of bread and two fish into enough food to feed the entire multitude (see John 6:1-14).

In the grand scheme of things, most consider faith to be an abstract notion. In the minds of practical thinkers, the concept of believing in the impossible is senseless. However, the people of God are propelled to a higher calling. We are pulled to a deeper level of faith that tunnels beneath obstacles, and provides answers to life's challenging questions; this is the kind of faith that connects us to solutions. In instances where there are no financial or physical resources left in the gas tank of life, we discover that irrational faith will take us to the next filling station. In her song entitled "Fragile Heart", Yolanda Adams reminds us that God is waiting to help you put the broken pieces back together again. ***God is ready, willing and, as my mother would say, "able to see you through"***. It is my prayer that you will gain strength and inspiration from this book. There is also a hope that you will be empowered to seize the blessing that lies beyond the breakthrough of your circumstance. Come along and discover the power of irrational faith.

Chapter One

BE CONVERTED

"By faith the prostitute Rahab, because she welcomed the spies, was not killed with those who were disobedient." (Heb. 11:31)

"If you declare with your mouth Jesus is Lord, and believe in your heart that God raised him from the dead, you will be saved." (Rom. 10:9)

Old belief: "All you need to do is quote Romans 10:9, and you will be saved."

Irrational faith begins with a confession and an obsession. There must be a confession that Jesus is Lord, and a whole heart, fixated belief that God raised Him from the dead. "Love the Lord your God with all your heart and with all your soul and with your entire mind and with all your strength," (Mk 12:30). In other words, we have to become a sell-out for Jesus. When we become sell-outs, it means that we have made up our minds to betray the world, avoiding anything that signals a potential roadblock to our freedom in Christ. We are no longer a slave to the bondage of sin.

Question

"What must I do to be saved?"

Rahab's Conversion

Rahab is a name that we would probably least expect to find engraved in the annals of history among great faith heroes. She was a woman who dishonored herself with sexual sin. In spite of her past history, God used her mightily; she became a vehicle of breakthrough for the children of Israel.

After surviving the death of Moses and wandering in the wilderness for forty years, the Israelites finally arrived at the promised land of Canaan. Joshua was the new leader, and the mission was to send out scouts to spy on the fortified City of Jericho. God's miraculous providence is worked through Rahab, a former prostitute, who owned a house that was strategically located on top of the city wall; it was used to hide spies. The king was informed of this, and ordered her to turn over the men to the authorities. With fear and reverence for the God of Israel, Rahab made a decision to lie in support of the mission, which ultimately helped the spies to avoid being killed.

In exchange for her own life, and the lives of her family members, she struck a deal with the spies to keep silent about the plan. Rahab was told that she would be saved from the coming judgment of God upon sinful people if she displayed this scarlet cord. They hung a scarlet cord from her window as a sign that she was on the Lord's side. As a result, she and her entire household were spared during the Israelite invasion of Jericho. ***The scarlet cord represents Emmanuel, the blood of Jesus Christ that saves every sinner from the penalty and judgment of sin.***

This act was providential for three reasons. First, it fulfills the promise of God to the children of Israel.

"So the LORD gave Israel all the land He had sworn to give their ancestors, and they took possession of it and settled there. The LORD gave them rest on every side, just as He had sworn to their ancestors. Not one of their enemies withstood them; the LORD gave all their enemies into their hands. Not one of all the LORD's good promises to Israel failed; everyone was fulfilled," (Josh. 21:43-45).

Second, it is an example of what sinners must do to be converted.

"Come to me, all you who are weary and burdened, and I will give you rest. Take my yoke upon you and learn from me, for I am gentle and humble in heart, and you will find rest for your souls. For my yoke is easy and my burden is light," (Matt. 11:28-30).

Finally, it represents the reward that is promised to all sinners who surrender from a life of sin to be converted.

"Come now, let us reason together," says the LORD. "Though your sins are like scarlet, they shall be as white as snow; though they are red as crimson, they shall be like wool," (Isa. 1:18).

Breakthrough

Rahab's surrender and initiative led to her breakthrough; the breakthrough led to the blessing. She had been looking for a way of escape from a life of sin and shame. Deep down inside, she knew that there had to be a change. She was moved by the Holy Spirit; yes, the Spirit was indeed at work, even with this stained woman. In her own way, she accepts a new way of life and direction. She made a decision to stand up for the cause of the holy and the sanctified God of Israel, the one who never sleeps or slumbers. ***Irrational faith is determined by our readiness to be a part of God's plan.*** This is often done in the face of uncertainty. Rahab gambled on the belief that she would be rescued; the result was her conversion and deliverance.

The Blessing

The blessings of Jericho lay immediately beyond the gate of the city. It was a sunny place below sea level, supplying good rainfall, an abundance of fresh water and good soil. God gives His children what they need the most. ***We are the redeemed of the Lord and the sheep of the Lord's pasture.*** One songwriter wrote; 'Let the redeemed of the Lord say so." Psalm

107:2 states: "If you are saved, you ought to say it loud, because God has indeed saved you from the hand of the enemy." Walk in your conversion!

Your Mouth

"That if you confess with your mouth Jesus is Lord, and believe in your heart that God raised him from the dead, you will be saved," (Rom. 10:9). ***The mouth is the place where the blessing gets enforced; it becomes the vehicle of abundance.*** It is critical for believers to always speak positive words of life. Amidst death, doubt and destruction, the words of faith must be spoken. ***This means that we must keep our mouths free from things that will block the breakthrough and the blessing.*** Profanity, gossiping, lying and talking negatively will hinder the good things that God has in store for you. "For the LORD God is a sun and shield; the LORD bestows favor and honor; no good thing does He withhold from those whose walk is blameless," (Ps. 84:11). It is with our mouth that we confess and are saved.

Your Heart

Our heart is the place where we believe and are justified. As the scripture says, "Anyone who trusts in Him will never be put to shame," (Rom. 10:11). For there is no difference between Jew and Gentile, the same Lord is Lord of all and richly blesses all who call on Him, for "Everyone who calls on the name of the Lord will be saved," (Rom. 10:13). Heart belief gives us victory over and above any challenge we may face in life. ***The heart is the center of our being; it is the core of our spirit and emotions.***

It is the very storehouse of all our beliefs. "Above all else, guard your heart, for it is the wellspring of life," (Prov. 4:23). The belief that is stored in our hearts becomes the foundation of our breakthrough.

Your Surrender

No one rolls out of bed with instant faith; it starts with a radical decision to allow God to jump-start our lives. Surrendering to God takes us into the spiritual realm. This is real conversion, without having all the answers. ***Breakthrough begins the moment we become transformed.*** The Apostle Paul says:

> "Therefore, I urge you, brothers, in view of God's mercy, to offer your bodies as living sacrifices, holy and pleasing to God—this is your spiritual act of worship. Do not conform any longer to the pattern of this world, but be transformed by the renewing of your mind. Then you will be able to test and approve what God's will is—His good, pleasing and perfect will," (Rom. 12:1-2).

Jesus states to Nicademus:

> "I tell you the truth, no one can enter the kingdom of God unless he is born of water and the Spirit. Flesh gives birth to flesh, but the Spirit gives birth to spirit. You

should not be surprised at my saying, 'you must be born again," (Jn. 3:5-7).

The blessing of salvation is freely given to anyone who is willing to allow the Holy Spirit the opportunity to transform them through a process that begins with complete surrender.

The Key

<u>Proclamation</u>

Public profession alone does not validate inward salvation; our salvation is prearranged through the sacrifice of Christ. "For those God foreknew He also predestined to be conformed to the image of His Son that He might be the firstborn among many brothers and sisters," (Rom. 8:29). Redemption is freedom from guilt and stain of sin. The profession of one's faith is an outward declaration of what has taken place in the heart of the believer, prior to the public announcement. Without reservation, I agree with the statement that says: "Anything other than true heart belief is only lip service." The heart is the place of justification. This heart validation makes us right in the eyesight of God; this corrective act amounts to our peace with God. "Consequently, you are no longer foreigners and strangers, but fellow citizens with God's people and also members of His household," (Eph. 2:19).

I would also add that this justification is the result of our faith in Christ, not the law. "So the law was our guardian until Christ came that we might be justified by faith," (Gal. 3:24). The bloodshed of Christ provided the perfect covering for our sins, beyond race, religion or creed. For this reason, there exists a new covenant of faith between the believer and Christ.

To be sure, this new covenant rests on the finished work of Christ. While being bruised, battered and blood-stained, at his last breath, He proclaimed to the world that He had indeed borne the penalty of sin for all of humanity. It was the profession of His finished earthly assignment that gives us access and authority to proclaim that we are indeed saved, sanctified and filled with the Holy Spirit. "When He had received the drink, Jesus said, 'It is finished'. With that, He bowed His head and gave up His spirit," (Jn 19:30).

Life Lesson

The early years of my life were the simplest; I was raised in a semi-religious environment where "God was God and besides Him, there was no other." I say semi-religious because my mother, an ardent churchgoer, trusted in God with her whole heart. In those days, my father did not attend church. Today, he faithfully serves as the chairman of the deacon board and spends just as much time in the house of the Lord as my mother. Praise God! My faith was also shaped by a highly-religious paternal grandmother and a maternal grandmother: Mom, Grandma and Momma were the three main players in my faith formation.

To make life simple, I chose to believe in the God of these three women. However, I wound up being confused because I had been programmed to believe that God was loving and, at the same time, wrathful. I had always been told that "He was good, and that He would make a way where there seemed to be no way." I felt misinformed and misguided at the same time. It was difficult for me to process God as being "stiff and terrible," yet merciful and forgiving; this perceived contradiction led to frustration.

A combination of Mom's, Grandma's and Momma's God caused me to rid myself of it all. I chose a path of independence because it was less frustrating; this was the beginning of the wonder years of my life. I wanted a taste of the "good life". These ladies had provided me with the perfect excuse to explore the world. I made a vow that I would experience many of the avenues that they had forbid me to travel.

It was commonplace in my neighborhood to steal candy from the local grocery store. Although I have never taken part in murder, rape or robbery, I was guilty of other so-called mischief. Stealing valve stem covers, unlawfully vandalizing school property, drinking and smoking cigarettes never seemed criminal.

Some of my closest childhood friends had chosen a life of delinquency, and were going through the court system with rapid speed. They had already become part of the juvenile justice system, and I was left with the option to join them in increasing the statistics. To be perfectly honest, I was running a close second; rebelliousness had become a part of my personality. It was as if I were running through an obstacle course with closed eyes.

After looking back on those years, I see that God has brought me through seen and unseen dangers. I was suddenly faced with a rude awakening. After living a life of rebellion and finding out that the world was not only a tough one, but criminal as well, my eyes were opened. The ultimate turning point for me, although I was only fifteen at the time, was learning that I was going to be a father.

As a young father, I learned the meaning of sacrifice. The track coach at my high school, after watching me run the meter tryouts, acknowledged my talent. Again, after I showed exceptional skill in the hurdles, he and I were even more convinced of my future as a track-and-field athlete however, it became a dream deferred. Instead of track, I had to choose a more sensible career—bag boy at the local grocery store. I had also discovered a hidden talent and love for the theater. I chose theater because acting came naturally for me; it was an opportunity to create my own environment. Acting was an avenue of expression to speak to the world and, at the same time, be recognized as a young man who would someday be a star. In jest, my dad would call me Richard Roundtree, a successful, famous African-American actor.

Needless to say, I had to put this part of my life on hold as well. Although starring in three major roles at my high school and being recognized for such, I realized that the glitz and glamour of the theater did not provide the financial resources necessary to support my new baby girl. I learned the meaning of sacrifice, humility and patience. However, it was necessary for me to travel the roads I traveled; God was developing my patience to face and endure my present task in the place where I now served.

Saved

There suddenly existed a whole new life for me in the church; the God of my mother and grandmothers was not as bad as I had imagined.

God suddenly became a God of mercy and forgiveness. It is Solomon who declares: "Train up a child in the way he should go and when he is old, he will not depart from it," (Prov. 22:6). For me, these words are so true. I must admit that the transitions from boyhood to fatherhood contributed to what I now believe are two of the strongest aspects of my personality, humility and patience. Therefore, I make it a priority to provide freedom to those who desire to be converted. Potential converts need space and grace to come to God on their own accord. "For I say, through the grace given to me, to everyone who is among you, not to think of himself more highly than he ought to think, but to think soberly, as God has dealt to each one a measure of faith," (Rom. 12:3) ***Complete surrender and total renewal is only achieved when we make up our minds that we will resist worldly pressure to conform.***

New Belief: "Therefore, if anyone is in Christ, the new creation has come: The old has gone, the new is here," (2 Cor. 5:17).

Remember

1- The scarlet cord represents Emmanuel, the blood of Jesus Christ.

2- Irrational faith is our readiness to be a part of God's plan.

3- We are the redeemed of the Lord and the sheep of the Lord's pasture.

4- The mouth is the place where the blessing gets enforced.

5- We must keep our mouths free from things that block the breakthrough and the blessing.

6- The heart is the core of our spirit and emotions.

7- Breakthrough begins at the moment of transformation.

8- Renewal is achievedwhen we resist worldly things.

Chapter Two

BE SURE

On the third day, Abraham looked up and saw the place in the distance. He said to his servants, "Stay here with the donkey while I and the boy go over there. We will worship and then we will come back to you," (Gen. 22:4-5)

Old Belief: "There is no hope."

The mark of true faith is exemplified when we are obedient to God's command. Abraham is the perfect model of this kind of faith. He trusted God with complete confidence, which resulted in a life of victory and blessings. He emerged out of every trial with the magnificent splendor of pure gold. These have come so that "the proven genuineness of your faith—of greater worth than gold, which perishes, even though refined by fire—may result in praise, glory and honor when Jesus Christ is revealed," (1 Pet. 1:7).

Question

"Are you willing to totally rely on God for the solution to your problem?"

<u>Promise</u>

At the age of ninety-nine, God reminded Abraham of the promise to give him a son. God also said to Abraham;

> "As for Sarai your wife, you are no longer to call her Sarai; her name will be Sarah. I will bless her and will surely give you a son by her. I will bless her so that she will be the mother of nations; kings of peoples will come from her." Abraham fell facedown; he laughed and said to himself, "Will a son be born to a man a hundred years old? Will Sarah bear a child at the age of ninety?" And Abraham said to God, "If only Ishmael might live under your blessing!" Then God said, "Yes, but your wife Sarah will bear you a son, and you will call him Isaac. I will establish my covenant with him as an everlasting covenant for his descendants after him," (Gen. 17:15-19).

<u>Test</u>

The ultimate test came when God asked Abraham to sacrifice Isaac. Sometime later, God tested Abraham.

> God said to him, "Abraham!" "Here I am," he replied. Then God said, "Take your son, your only son, whom you love—Isaac—and go to the region of Mariah. Sacrifice him there as a burnt offering on a mountain I will show you," (Gen. 22:2).

As one can imagine, this must have been the most agonizing moment in Abraham's life. However, this request warranted immediate action. Though he held cherished memories of more than twenty-one years of life, love, lessons and bonding with Isaac, Abraham moved without hesitation to carry out the mission of God. He was sure that God would not go back on the promise that was made to him.

> "Early the next morning, Abraham got up and loaded his donkey. He took with him two of his servants and his son Isaac. When he had cut enough wood for the burnt offering, he set out for the place God had told him about," (Gen. 22:3).

After three days' journey, he was able to work through the mental anguish of having to kill Isaac, and arrived at a conclusion that God was going to provide what he needed. Faith was at work in the heart and mind of Abraham. He believed in the process of what God was doing; God's rational is far beyond human reasoning. ***Irrational faith does not***

interfere with the process of God; neither does it attempt to rationalize kingdom business. However, it is confidence in what God will do.

> "By faith Abraham, when God tested him, offered Isaac as a sacrifice. He who had embraced the promises was about to sacrifice his one and only son, even though God had said to him, 'It is through Isaac that your offspring will be reckoned.' Abraham reasoned that God could even raise the dead, and so in a manner of speaking he did receive Isaac back from death," (Heb. 11:17-19).

> On the third day, Abraham looked up and saw the place in the distance. He said to his servants, "Stay here with the donkey while I and the boy go over there. We will worship and then we will come back to you," (Gen. 22:4-5).

Abraham's order to his servants to remain at the base of the mountain indicated that he understood that God was sovereign and completely in control. ***Irrational faith gives God complete control in every circumstance.***

> "Do not be anxious about anything, but in every situation, by prayer and petition, with thanksgiving, present your requests to God. And the peace of God, which

transcends all understanding, will guard your hearts and your minds in Christ Jesus," (Phil. 4:6-7).

Breakthrough

Giving God complete control takes us into personal breakthrough. Breakthrough begins in the spirit realm; we enter the spirit realm through worship. *Worship is the vehicle that places us on the other side of trouble.* The purpose of worship is to praise, exalt, honor, glorify and, ultimately, please God. Our worship to God also provides us with the way to escape from sin and temptation. *God requires our devotion through the act of humble submission.* Worship achieves this goal. "But he gives us more grace. That is why Scripture says: 'God opposes the proud but shows favor to the humble,'" (Jas 4:6).

Abraham needed to clear his mind, and the only way to do it was through worship! Setting up an alter to worship and praise God reinforced what he already knew. This act ensured that His faith stood firmly on the belief that through omniscient, omnipresent and omnipotent power, God would provide what he needed! Worship was the vehicle that he used to transport him to victory. In the midst of crisis, He trusted God with his whole heart, and received his breakthrough. *During critical life junctures and decisions, we must find a personal space, build a spiritual alter and worship God for the breakthrough!* Abraham's irrational faith accepted the miracle of Isaac being spared. In his mind, he put Isaac to death and resurrected him before he reached the mountaintop.

The critical question that challenges our faith is: What are we willing to put to death for the sake of pleasing God? The answer to this question should be everything!

> "For I am convinced that neither death nor life, neither angels nor demons, neither the present nor the future, nor any powers, neither height nor depth, nor anything else in all creation, will be able to separate us from the love of God that is in Christ Jesus our Lord," (Rom. 8:38-39).

<u>Response</u>

Abraham's response was immediate, which proved that God, not Isaac, was his first priority.

> "God himself will provide the lamb for the burnt offering, my son." And the two of them went on together. When they reached the place God had told him about, Abraham built an altar there and arranged the wood on it. He bound his son Isaac and laid him on the altar, on top of the wood. Then he reached out his hand and took the knife to slay his son," (Gen. 22:8-10).

God's purpose was for Jesus to be sacrificed for our redemption, not Isaac. Isaac was a preview of what would later be done through Christ. *Obeying God requires that we move forward with God's divine plan. There must be complete assurance and trust that God will finish what has been started in us.* "Being confident of this, that he who began a good work in you will carry it on to completion until the day of Christ Jesus," (Phil. 1:6). *Know that God can be trusted, and God's plan is always undergirded by two things: promise and provision.*

The Blessing

God promised Abraham that he would be the recipient of immeasurable blessings. He was directed by the Holy Spirit to follow God's agenda. God explained that favor will be granted to him and his household, which will overshadow past, present and future obstacles. These blessings are tucked away in the Abrahamic covenant, which consists of seven parts. The operative word in the statement of promise is the word "bless". It follows a series of "I will" statements that God speaks to Abraham.

> "The LORD had said to Abram, 'Go from your country, your people and your father's household to the land I will show you. I will make you into a great nation, and I will bless you; I will make your name great, and you will be a blessing. I will bless those who bless you, and

whoever curses you I will curse; and all peoples on earth will be blessed through you.' (Gen. 12:1-3).

Requirement

The sovereign road map that God was preparing for him required that he abandon current attachments to family, friends and the atmosphere of unholy deities: Abraham was commanded to move to an unknown place. ***Irrational faith requires movement without specified knowledge.*** However, the absence of knowledge is not the absence of planning and setting goals: it is being confident that God will provide an answer. This kind of faith is fueled by the belief that the things we desire will indeed take place.

Desire

God placed desire in the heart of Abraham through covenant relationship. This covenant relationship is established through faith and obedience which leads to righteousness.

> "Abraham was ninety-nine years old when he was circumcised, and his son Ishmael was thirteen; Abraham and his son Ishmael were both circumcised on that very day. And every male in Abraham's household, including those born in his household or bought from a foreigner, was circumcised with him," (Gen. 17:24-27).

Just as with Abraham, God places desire within us, shaping our heart through the Holy Spirit to desire righteous things. Through spiritual circumcision, the soul is separated from our sinful bodies. Spiritual circumcision takes place in the heart. ***The heart is where we are connected in covenant relationship with God, and faith unlocks the door to the provision of blessings stored in the covenant.*** "Therefore, if anyone is in Christ, the new creation has come: The old has gone, the new is here!" (2 Cor. 5:17). "No, a person is a Jew who is one inwardly; and circumcision is circumcision of the heart, by the Spirit, not by the written code. Such a person's praise is not from other people, but from God," (Rom. 2:29).

Leaving

My desire to fulfill the call to ministry was indeed fueled by extraordinary faith, to leave a place of familiarity and comfort. In 1989, I enrolled at Howard Divinity School; that year was one of the most exciting and challenging years of my life. I preached my initial sermon, graduated from Norfolk State University and married my soul mate, Paula Jean. I then ventured off to Washington D.C., with a great deal of uncertainty. Leaving my new bride shortly after our honeymoon, not having full-time employment or a place for us to live, created great anxiety. My move to Washington was truly a move of faith: It was like the time God told Abraham to go to a place with which he was unfamiliar. (See Genesis 12:1.) The only assurance I had at the time was that I knew God had called me to do ministry in an unfamiliar place. Shortly after I completed orientation in Mays Hall at the Divinity

School, my need for housing was answered with an offer of a room upstairs in the same building, where I stayed for approximately two weeks. Having to share a room and be away from my new bride made it difficult for me to remain focused. After many days and nights in prayer about a job for my wife, I was happy to learn that she had been offered a GS 7 position at the Washington Navy Yard; she would be joining me in two weeks.

However, I was still faced with the problem of not having a place for us to live. Although the dormitory was coed, it was obvious that we could not make a home there. Determined to keep the faith, I continued my search, and eventually found a cozy little apartment away from the drug zone.

As a wedding gift, my wife and I had received a large sum of money, which we decided to use for relocation expenses. However, we did not realize that the cost of living in Washington was so expensive. Our little wedding nest egg vanished in a matter of days; but no matter how dark the way seems, God always comes through. We met a realtor who was extremely generous. He allowed us to live rent-free in one of the condominiums he owned for the first month, and deferred payment of the security deposit for one year. In the same week, I was offered a part-time job at one of our denominational churches. My wife joined me a week later in what was to become our happy home. "Take delight in the LORD, and He will give you the desires of your heart. Commit your way to the LORD; trust in Him and He will do this," (Ps 37:4-5).

The Key

<u>Provision</u>

On an ordinary hill in a place called Moriah, something extraordinary happened. Isaac, who was once bound and restricted, was set free. As a result, Abraham named the place Jehovah Jireh; this became the mountain of provision. It was here that Abraham's faith was confirmed. **God appoints seasons when we are blessed with uncommon favor in unusual circumstances.** God was moved by Abraham's unshakable, irrational faith:

> "As it is written: 'I have made you a father of many nations.' He is our father in the sight of God, in whom he believed—the God who gives life to the dead and calls into being things that were not," (Rom. 4:17).

Life Lesson

<u>"Scarcity, the Mother of all Inventions"</u>

My maternal grandmother, Maggie Taylor, was an expert at making something out of nothing. I have fond memories of being in the kitchen with her on rainy days while she prepared good food. One of my favorite snacks was glazed donuts made from canned biscuits. During thunderstorms, she would say: ***"Be quiet, and let the good Lord do His work."*** So in great, but silent, anticipation, I watched as she formed each biscuit in the shape of a small donut, slowly dropping them into a large, deep cast iron skillet full of hot lard. When the cooked dough floated to the surface, it signified that the donuts were ready. Then she would dip the hot, crispy donut into a bowl of syrupy glaze, made from a mixture of sugar and water. The final step was adding cinnamon to half the batch.

I remember the sweet taste of snow cream, made only from the second wave of a snowstorm. She would place one of her large cooking pots atop the awning to catch the snow. After retrieving the pot, she would immediately add sugar, canned milk, a pinch of salt and vanilla extract. It was the best snow cream in town.

From my grandmother, I learned a few things about cooking that have helped me to understand why I love good food on rainy days; but the deeper lesson was what appears to be insignificant to others can be transformed into a miracle through the power of God. Today, I still believe in the power of God to make something out of nothing.

> "Jesus then took the loaves, gave thanks, and distributed to those who were seated as much as they wanted. He did the same with the fish. When they had all had enough to eat, he said to his disciples, 'Gather the pieces that are left over. Let nothing be wasted,'" (Jn 6:11-12).

New Belief: "Who dares to despise the day of small things, since the seven eyes of the Lord that range throughout the earth will rejoice when they see the chosen capstone in the hand of Zerubbabel," (Zec. 4:10).

Remember

1- True faith is obedience to God's commands.

2- Irrational faith does not interfere with the process of God.

3- Irrational faith always gives God complete control.

4- Worship places us on the other side of trouble.

5- God requires devotion through humble submission.

6- Abraham cleared his mind through worship.

7- At critical life junctures, find a personal space and build a spiritual alter.

8- Trust that God will complete what was started in us.

9- God's plan is always undergirded by promises and provision.

10- Irrational faith is movement without specified knowledge.

11- The heart is the place of covenant relationship.

12- God gives uncommon favor in unusual circumstances.

13- Grandma Maggie Taylor said: *"Be quiet, and let the good Lord is do His work."*

Chapter Three

BE PRAYERFUL

Then they said to the king, "Daniel, who is one of the exiles from Judah, pays no attention to you, Your Majesty, or to the decree you put in writing. He still prays three times a day." (Dan. 6:13)

He replied, "This kind can come out only by prayer." (Mk 9:29)

Old Belief: "God doesn't hear my prayers."

Many people buy into the common belief that their prayers are not heard; this leads to negative thinking, which ultimately limits positive thoughts and positive actions. Without belief in God's power, or the ability to tap into God's storehouse of resources, we can be totally disempowered. Tangible things that we have relied on in the past to get us through difficult circumstances may not always be available. ***The good news is belief is always available, providing constant direction to our lives.*** When confronted with a problem, we make a subconscious decision to believe or not to believe. What we believe, whether good or bad, becomes the center of our world. It is the filter that we use to measure everything around us; everything falls under the acid test of our belief system. ***The truth is God has already provided answers to our most pressing issues through the shed blood of Jesus Christ.*** The solution is right under our noses, but all too often, God's divine voice is silenced by anxiety, doubt and fear. ***A famous quote from my mother during distressing times is, "God sees, knows and cares".*** If there is ever a time when our view of life becomes obstructed by the debris of difficult problems, we must remember that God has an excellent track record of past blessings and miracles. At the wedding of Cana, Jesus turned water into wine:

> "And the master of the banquet tasted the water that had been turned into wine. He did not realize where it had come from, though the servants who had drawn the water knew. Then he called the bridegroom aside," (Jn. 2:9).

He also healed the man at the pool of Bethesda. Then Jesus said to him, "Get up! Pick up your mat and walk.' At once the man was cured; he picked up his mat and walked. The day on which this took place was a Sabbath," (Jn. 5:8-9).

Question

Are you willing to engage in regular and consistent prayer to obtain power for the breakthrough?

Daniel's Prayer

Practice, Purpose, Direction

Daniel was a man on a mission, interceding in prayer on behalf of his people. Despite the law not to pray, He believed that God not only heard his prayers, but would solve the crisis of the nation as well. Even after being thrown in the lion's den, he continued to pray. His constant habit of prayer kept Him connected to the power of God's deliverance. His captors understood the impact of being thrown in the lion's den; they knew the power of the hungry lions. The bite pressure of a lion's jaw renders approximately 945 pounds of pressure per square inch, which would amount to 700 pounds of crushing power. With such force, Daniel would surely be destroyed. He, in an act of irrational, faith-filled defiance, continued to pray in the face of ferocious lions. He understood the impact of having irrational faith in the power of God, regardless of the circumstance. He also knew Jesus, the Lion of Judah; both he and Jesus were direct descendants of the tribe of Judah. His knowledge of the power of the coming Messiah compelled him to maintain an intense regiment of prayer. In the midst of trouble, we must rely on the knowledge that Jesus, the Lion of Judah, dwells within our sanctified souls! ***Irrational faith keeps us mindful that we should never panic, because God is always in control.*** "You, dear children, are from God and have overcome them, because the one who is in you is greater than the one who is in the world," (1 Jn 4:4).

Practicing consistent and regular prayer expanded Daniel's faith and abolished His fear. The result was His breakthrough, which led to the blessing of deliverance from the jaws of hungry lions. "Therefore I tell you, whatever you ask for in prayer, believe that you have received it, and it will be yours," (Mk 11:24). Paul reinforced Daniel's prophesy, in Daniel 9:24-27, concerning Jesus by proclaiming that through grace we are made righteous.

Paul says:

> "For I am not ashamed of the gospel, because it is the power of God that brings salvation to everyone who believes: first to the Jew, then to the Gentile. For in the gospel the righteousness of God is revealed—a righteousness that is by faith from first to last, just as it is written: The righteous will live by faith," (Rom. 1:16-17).

His purpose

Daniel prayed to demonstrate his devotion to God. It helped him to gain a depth of understanding that would later prove to be very powerful. Other reasons were for the release of his people, who were being held captive, the rebuilding of Jerusalem and the temple. He made a specific request for God's mercy, forgiveness and deliverance. He understood that constant prayer would ensure God's presence in his life; prayer kept him connected to God.

His direction

During prayer, Daniel always bowed in the direction of Jerusalem. Praying toward Jerusalem kept the Jews focused on God, the direction of deliverance at the time of breakthrough. He prophesied that Jesus would come and deal with the problem of sin and evil by restoring the City of God. "Know and understand this: from the time the word goes out to restore and rebuild Jerusalem until the Anointed One, the ruler, comes, there will be seven 'sevens,' and sixty-two 'sevens.' It will be rebuilt with streets and a trench, but in times of trouble," (Dan. 9:25).

Your Direction

Always pray in the direction of God's will. Praying in the direction of God's will is praying according to God's written word and purpose. "And we know that in all things God works for the good of those who love him, who have been called according to His purpose," (Rom. 8:28).

As faith-filled believers, we are instructed to memorize God's promises and follow the conditions set forth to receive the blessings.

> "He will love you, bless you and multiply you. He will also bless the fruit of your womb and the fruit of your ground, your grain and your wine and your oil, the increase of your herds and the young of your flock, in the land that He swore to your fathers to give you," (Deut.7: 13).

Our faith must be solid and unwavering; irrational faith has no place for doubting the undeniable power of God. **Faith and doubt cannot dwell in the same house.** Irrational, unrelenting faith is increased by studying the word. ***This radical method of study is achieved by writing out the scriptures, reading them aloud and speaking solutions to our current conditions.*** This should take place before you enter the House of God. "Do your best to present yourself to God as one approved, a worker who does not need to be ashamed and who correctly handles the word of truth," (2 Tim. 2:15).

As the preacher delivers the message on Sunday morning, our response should be a resounding echo of Amen! Amen simply means that we agree with the preached word. ***The spoken word is a confirmation of what you have heard and received from the voice of God during your personal study time.*** As we study, listen and receive God's word, we will gain wisdom and insight. "Consequently, faith comes from hearing the message, and the message is heard through the word about Christ," (Rom. 10:17).

Disciples' Faith

The ninth chapter of Mark describes a man who needed a miracle for his son. He asks the disciples for help, but they could not deliver a cure. One would think this would have been an easy task because of the amount of time they spent with Jesus. After all, they were unique and set apart in an intimate, personal relationship with the Lord. In reality, they could not deliver the cure because of their lack of faith. They lacked faith and spiritual power because of their limited time in prayer. They walked with him, but did not possess power for the breakthrough.

The man with the sick son said to Jesus: "And they could not," (Mk 9:18). The disciples were unable to heal this boy because of insufficient spiritual power: In this instance, the devil's power trumped God's power. The problem was not with God, but with the missed opportunity of the disciples to take full advantage of what Jesus had offered. They had just witnessed the transfiguration, and forgot the miraculous power of God on the mountain. They lost sight of the vision of hope and belief that is possible through the power of Jesus. He rebuked their doubt, and called them a faithless generation. "You unbelieving generation, how long shall I stay with you? How long shall I put up with you? Bring the boy to me," (Mk 9:19).

Life's many distractions can limit our spiritual vision. "Such a person is double-minded and unstable in all they do," (Jas 1:8). ***A fundamental*** *problem with breakthrough power is unstable, inconsistent and wavering faith.* Jesus reminds us that: "The worries of this life, the deceitfulness of wealth and the desires for other things come in and choke the word, making it unfruitful," (Mk 4:19). ***Don't lose sight of the blessing that lies beyond the breakthrough.*** Be aware of life's trivial pursuits and worries; these are the little rocks that cloud our vision and steal our joy.

Breakthrough

There will be times in life when God's riches are not visible to the natural eye. ***Just remember that our breakthrough is determined by what we see and believe in the spiritual realm.*** The Apostle Paul reminds us that the breakthrough comes from above. "And my God will meet all your needs, according to the riches of his glory in Christ Jesus," (Phil. 4:19). ***The breakthrough comes from the God of glory, who has all power. Irrational faith confirms that the blessing is right before us, even when it is not detectible.***

> "For though we live in the world, we do not wage war as the world does. The weapons we fight with are not the weapons of the world. On the contrary, they have divine power to demolish strongholds. That the weapons of our warfare are not carnal, but mighty through God," (2 Cor. 10:3-4).

Faith emerges as victorious in every circumstance; therefore, it must be radical and unyielding!

The Blessing

Practice, Purpose, Direction

Irrational faith exercises the practice, purpose and direction of prayer. Prayer should be a regular part of our lives, if we expect to walk in deliverance and abundance. **Begin a life of prayer by setting aside regular period at the same time every day.** Start out by praying fifteen minutes a day at a time that is best suited for your schedule; this may be morning or afternoon. The posture of prayer is not as important as the commitment. It has been explained that in order to get a fervent prayer through to heaven, one must be on bending knees. God is more concerned with our commitment to prayer rather than the position we use while praying. Prayer can be rendered while walking the dog or mowing the lawn.

Purpose

The purpose of prayer is to keep us in constant, uninterrupted communication with God. Daniel refused to eat the king's food, because he knew that it was a menu that ran contrary to Jewish dietary laws. The food had also been offered to idols; partaking in these delicacies would tie him to the demands of the flesh. Daniel understood that he could only serve one God. His service had to be directed toward the holy God of the mountain. *Like Daniel, we should pray with the purpose of staying free from a life of contamination of the mind, body and spirit.*

Direction

Praying in the direction of God lines us up to be led by the Holy Spirit. "But when he, the Spirit of truth, comes, he will guide you into all the truth. He will not speak on his own; he will speak only what he hears, and he will tell you what is yet to come," (Jn 16:13). The way to receive direction from God is to ask.

> "If any of you lacks wisdom, you should ask God, who gives generously to all without finding fault, and it will be given to you. But when you ask, you must believe and not doubt...that person should not expect to receive anything from the Lord," (Jas 1:5-7).

This is where we receive God's guidance, clearly distinguishing God's voice from all others. *The voice of the Lord is distinct and separate from the noise of the world. As we study the word, our ears and eyes will be opened.* "Your word is a lamp for my feet, a light on my path," (Ps. 119:105). *Talking with God keeps God's will at the forefront of our priorities.* Prayer helps us experience the presence of our universal Creator. This experience alone creates personal transformation, which takes our faith to a new level of spiritual awareness. "But seek first His kingdom and His righteousness, and all these things will be given to you as well," (Matt. 6:33).

The Key

Walking with God gives us power for the breakthrough; this power comes by spending time in prayer. *The time spent in prayer should also be done alongside others who have submitted themselves to the discipline of regular prayer.*

Life lesson

As a young man, my mother and I attended early Sunday morning prayer meetings at our church. The small weekly gathering of dedicated saints was a safe place for me to share my testimony about God's goodness. In tough times, my mother would say to me: **"Somehow, God will make a way out of no way."** I sought the wisdom of seasoned churchgoers, because I believed they possessed deep wisdom and spiritual knowledge. It proved to be extremely beneficial, as I received direction for many of the challenges that I would experience down the road.

One such challenge occurred during the week of May 10, 1999, at my highest point of burnout. I felt horrible about my church situation. Many of the programs initiated when I arrived were now cancelled, or on the brink of being shut down. I was challenged by a very small, influential group at my church to come up with solutions to the problems. They were not the most evil people one could imagine: however, on the list of passivity, they ranked very high. Whether true or not, in my mind, they were as much the cause of the decline of membership as I was. It became very clear to me one night, while praying, that I was passing through the stages of grief. The loss of a loved one is not the only time that one experiences grief; grief can be felt when one loses something significant. Julie Axelrod comments on Elizabeth Kubler Ross's grief model in an article entitled: *5 stages of Loss and Grief:* "depression is a sort of acceptance with emotional attachment. It's natural to feel sadness and regret, fear, uncertainty, etc. It shows that the person has at least begun to accept the reality." The five stages of grief are denial and isolation, anger, bargaining, depression and acceptance. I was at stage four, depression, about to enter stage five, acceptance.

I was coming to terms that I had failed at successfully growing my church. A dying church in many ways meant professional and personal death. It represented professional death because I had not fully accomplished what I set out to do in the name of social justice for marginalized people; it was a deep, personal sorry. I also feared that I would not be able to financially provide for my family. The greatest challenge for the remainder of my tenure was to be patient and confident that God would provide what I needed. I knew my survival would be determined by clear guidance and direction. Needless to say, I resorted to what I learned in those fervent prayer meetings at church. Those meetings taught me to trust in God with my whole heart in distressing times. My personal prayer time became the vehicle of relief I needed for clarity and vision for where God would lead me in the next stage of my journey. Prayer helped me to remain calm during this difficult time, which led to a solid decision to later move on. ***When we engage in the habit of prayer, our faith***

becomes operational. The result is rock-solid trust in the power of God; you believe that anything is possible. "Therefore, confess your sins to each other and pray for each other so that you may be healed. The prayer of a righteous person is powerful and effective," (Jas 5:16).

New Belief: "And my God will meet all your needs according to the riches of His glory in Christ Jesus," (Phil. 4:19).

Remember

1- Belief always provides constant direction for our lives.

2- God has provided answers through the shed blood of Christ.

3- A famous quote from my mom : "God, sees, knows and cares."

4- Memorize God's promises and follow the conditions.

5- Write out the scripture, and speak aloud to your current condition.

6- Daniel continued to pray, in the face of ferocious lions.

7- Daniel knew the impact of prayer, despite the circumstance.

8- Jesus is the Lion of Judah.

9- The Lion of Judah dwells within our sanctified soul!

10- God is always in control of the situation.

11- Don't lose sight of the blessing.

12- Breakthrough happens first in the spirit realm.

13- Breakthrough comes from the God of glory.

14- Irrational faith confirms the reality of non-detectable blessings.

15- Victorious faith is radical and unyielding!

16- Set aside a regular period at the same time every day to pray.

17- Live free of contamination to the mind, body and spirit.

18- Pray in the direction of God's will.

19- The Lord's voice is different from the noise of the world.

20- As we study the Word, our ears and eyes will be opened.

21- Pray with others who are disciplined in the art of prayer.

22- My mother said: "Somehow, God would make a way out of no way."

23- Prayer makes our faith operational.

Chapter Four

BE PERSISTENT

"By faith Noah, when warned about things not yet seen, in holy fear built an ark to save his family. By his faith, he condemned the world and became heir of the righteousness that is in keeping with faith," (Heb. 11:7).

"Since they could not get him to Jesus because of the crowd, they made an opening in the roof above Jesus and, after digging through it, lowered the mat the paralyzed man was laying on,"(Mk 2:4).

Old Belief: "I don't know if I can make it."

In his book entitled *Disciplines of the Spirit*, the great theologian and poet Howard Thurman states: "At the core of life is a hard purposefulness, a determination to live. Commitment is a theme that is as ancient as the self-consciousness of man." I would also add that commitment is central to purpose and the core of persistence. ***When we make up our minds that we will take on the relentless pursuit of a task, nothing will be able to deter us.***

In the Christian church, we often quote: "No weapon forged against you will prevail, and you will refute every tongue that accuses you. This is the heritage of the servants of the LORD, and this is their vindication from me, declares the LORD," (Isa. 54:17). ***There must be a determination to fulfill the destiny that God has placed before us. This will require persistent faith. It requires a faith that dwells in the excess, one that believes in the overflow of blessings.*** "Now to Him who is able to do immeasurably more than all we ask or imagine, according to His power that is at work within us," (Eph. 3:20).

Question

Can you reach your destination in the face of adversity?

<u>Noah's Persistence</u>

Noah is the faith hero who stands out for his obedience to God. While being mocked and opposed in a godless society, he displayed steadfast obedience and unwavering faith. In preparation for a magnificent flood, God told him to build an ark. According to Genesis 6:15, the size of this mighty ship was 450 feet long, 75 feet wide and 45 feet high. It took many years and a whole lot of determination, to build the mighty vessel.

Through negativity, Noah persisted: His irrational faith was undergirded by righteousness before the God of promise. By any standard, Noah would be classified as a standout because he marched to the drumbeat of God. In an atmosphere of riotous living, he was determined to stand firmly on what he believed. Noah believed that God would keep the promise and not waver.

The God I'm describing is the God of uppercase G. The God of uppercase G is the true God; everyone else during this time followed the god of lowercase g. I say lowercase to emphasize their level of deep sin. They served the gods of their own lustful desires. Those so-called little g gods had no credibility, but the God of big G has a reputation to uphold. This reputation is one that promises direction and wisdom. The end result was Noah finding favor with God because of his remarkable, persistent faith. He and his entire household were saved, and received a tremendous storehouse of blessed abundance. That's good news!

> "Trust in the LORD and do good; dwell in the land and enjoy safe pasture. Take delight in the LORD, and He will give you the desires of your heart. Commit your way to the LORD; trust in Him and He will do this: He will make your righteous reward shine like the dawn, your vindication like the noonday sun," (Ps 37:3-6).

Breakthrough

Noah's breakthrough reward was a solid rock of blessing and promise. God told Noah and his sons they were to be fruitful and multiply. They were also given dominion over every animal that roamed the earth. God also explained:

> "This is the sign of the covenant I am making between me and you and every living creature with you, a covenant for all generations to come: I have set my rainbow in the clouds, and it will be the sign of the covenant between me and the earth. Whenever I bring clouds over the earth and the rainbow appears in the clouds, I will remember my covenant between me and you and all living creatures of every kind. Never again will the waters become a flood to destroy all life. Whenever the rainbow appears in the clouds, I will see it and remember the everlasting covenant between God and all living creatures of every kind on the earth," (Gen. 9:12-16).

Four Persistent Friends

The four friends in Mark Chapter 2 wanted to get their friend to Jesus, but could not because the crowd blocked the door to the house where Jesus was speaking. With extraordinary faith and determination, they were able to move beyond the obstacle that kept them from reaching their ultimate destination. Verse 4 states: "Since they could not get him to Jesus because of the crowd, they made an opening in the roof above Jesus by digging through it and then lowered the mat the man was lying on."

Miracle

Like Noah, the four friends were unaware of how God would move, in spite of the closed door, they exercised determined, irrational faith and received the miraculous, healing power of Jesus. They dug through grass, beams and clay to get their friend to Jesus. Their persistence resulted in a man being able to receive the grace of God, the forgiveness of sins, and mental, emotional and physical healing. This is a clear example of how breakthrough irrational faith seizes the blessing beyond the bearer. This is the kind of faith that is saturated with determination.

The Blessing

The blessing was a cooperative effort of men who displayed dogged determination to put the man in the place of his destiny and divine sanction. *The map of our destiny has already been sketched. Through anguish, pain and problems, the blessing must be pursued and seized with senseless, inconceivable, knuckle-grinding fearlessness!*

God's Voice

Hearing God's voice requires that we take bold steps in the breakthrough process. These steps include avoiding people, places and things that hinder our relationship and fellowship with Jesus. Doing this helps us to develop clear recognition of how God is directing our steps.

Don't allow anything to block the tailor-made blessings that God has stored up for us.

Spiritual Abundance

Spiritual abundance is the invisible harvest of blessings. When it appears that this treasure is not readily available, again remember that it is always stored in glory. "And my God will meet all your needs according to the riches of His glory in Christ Jesus," (Phil. 4:19). ***Harvesting spiritual abundance is cultivating the power that God has placed inside of us.*** It is the vast reservoir of mental, physical and emotional gifts and talents that lie just beneath the surface. The apostle Paul told Timothy to ripen the seed that lies within:

> "For this reason, I remind you to fan into flame the gift of God, which is in you through the laying on of my hands. For the Spirit God gave us does not make us timid, but gives us power, love and self-discipline," (2 Tim. 1:6-7).

Stirring our God-given gift pulls down our harvest of blessings.

Access

God has provided doors of access and opportunity for us. "I know your deeds. See, I have placed before you an open door that no one can shut. I know that you have little strength, yet you have kept my word and have not denied my name," (Rev.3:8). ***The goal for every believer is to keep these doors open and available to the free flow of blessings.*** This is achieved by reading the Word. Breakthrough blessings require that we consistently place the Word in our hearts, and confess God's name with our tongues. (See: Prov. 18:21.) ***Studying God's word and confessing life-giving affirmations in a dying situation enables us to see obstacles and move beyond them.***

In his book entitled *The Power of the Pew*, Franklyn Richardson states, ***"The open door represents unrestricted, unlimited, unrestrained and unfettered possibilities."*** This is an example of blessings beyond the breakthrough. Remember that behind every door of opportunity lies the ultimate gift and the prize possession, Jesus Christ. "For God so loved the world that He gave His only begotten Son, that whoever believes in Him should not perish but have everlasting life," (Jn 3:16).

Accept the fact that although we don't deserve it, God is "looking beyond our faults and providing us with the blessings that we need." "But he said to me, my grace is sufficient for you, for my power is made perfect in weakness. Therefore I will boast all the more gladly about my weaknesses, so that Christ's power may rest on me," (2 Cor.12:9).

The Key

The key to receiving both the breakthrough and the blessing is giving Jesus access into our hearts. "Here I am. I stand at the door and knock. If anyone hears my voice and opens the door, I will come in and eat with him, and he with me," (Rev. 3:20). Be faithful unto death, and He will give you a crown of life! Richardson says: ***"Faith is developed on stormy days behind closed doors."*** Storms are opportunities for growth: growth is achieved through the spiritual disciplines of fasting, praying, studying and solitude. "Not only so, but we also glory in our sufferings, because we know that suffering produces perseverance; perseverance, character; and character, hope," (Rom. 5:3-4). ***Regardless of age, opportunity, rank or social status, God will perform miracles beyond our imagination.*** The power that works within us is the Holy Spirit. Someone coined a phrase: "Don't confine Him to the guest room." When interpreted, this means that we must not compartmentalize the Holy Spirit to certain parts of our lives; instead, we must allow Him the freedom to have complete access in all areas. This is the key to the breakthrough and the blessing. "But you will receive power when the Holy Spirit comes on you; and you will be my witnesses in Jerusalem, and in all Judea and Samaria, and to the ends of the earth," (Acts 1:8). ***Irrational faith is the persistence and the belief in what God can do, in the face of impossible odds!***

Life Lesson

<u>Facing fears and Finding answers</u>

I believe it is a natural human tendency to avoid difficulty; to be quite honest, it's not altogether a bad thing. Nevertheless, when it is apparent that we are already in a tight place, or if difficulty finds its way into our present situation, decide to stand firm. The Word of God reminds us to be resilient.

> "Therefore, my dear brothers and sisters, stand firm. Let nothing move you. Always give yourselves fully to the

work of the Lord, because you know that your labor in the Lord is not in vain," (1 Cor. 15:58).

Fears

Until now, I have never admitted publicly that I feared being voted out of my church by hostile congregants. This fear had more to do with my own imagination than reality. Nevertheless, it caused me to avoid the tough issues. Today, I accept full responsibility for my fears and with careful analysis, I've concluded that my fear was the result of witnessing church hostility over the years. At any rate, I decided to confront the problem head-on. This has helped me face my tendency to be evasive in other areas of my life. ***The best way to confront any problem is with persistent and determined faith.***

Answers

Contrary to popular belief, answers are not always divine revelations. Sometimes we entertain the romantic notion that answers will be revealed by some "booming, sky-cracking" event. ***Answers are often right under our noses.*** We often miss them because we are preoccupied with acquiring wealth, status and work. Over involvement in these areas will cause us not to hear God's voice. ***I have discovered that answers become clear and more obvious through constant contact and communication with the sovereign Lord.***

My paternal grandmother, Mary Jones, used to say, ***"Sugar, you need to fast, pray, and read the Word of God."*** The apostle Paul says,

"The weapons we fight with are not the weapons of the world. On the contrary, they have divine power to demolish strongholds. We demolish arguments and every pretension that sets itself up against the knowledge of God, and we take captive every thought to make it obedient to Christ," (2 Cor. 10:4-5).

I believe that through devotions to God, we can accomplish what we have set out to do.

New Belief: "I can do all things through Christ who gives me strength," (Phil. 4:13).

Remember

1- Make up your mind that nothing will be able to deter you.

2- Be determined to fulfill your God-given destiny.

3- The map of our destiny has already been sketched.

4- Exclude anything that hinders your fellowship with Jesus.

5- Don't allow anything to block your tailor-made blessings.

6- Cultivate the power that God has placed inside of you.

7- Stirring our gift pulls down the harvest of blessings.

8- Keep the doors of blessings open and available.

9- Paul told Timothy to ripen the seed that was inside of him.

10- Confess life by giving affirmations in a dying situation.

11- "The open door represents unlimited possibilities."

12- God provides us with what we need.

13- "Faith is developed on stormy days behind closed doors."

14- God will perform miracles beyond our imagination.

15- Irrational faith believes God, despite the odds!

16- Confront all problems with determined faith.

17- The answers are right under your nose.

18- Answers are clear through communication with God.

19- Grandma Mary Jones said: "Sugar, you need to fast, pray, and read the Word of God."

20- Devotion to God helps us to accomplish goals.

Chapter Five

BE MOBILE

For she said, "If I just touch his clothes, I will be healed," (Mk 5:28).

Old Belief: "I'm stuck."

Everyone has a unique story; it represents both our history and our future; These stories are grounded in a collection of images, ideas, habits, morals and beliefs that make up the total person. The sums of all of these parts become the lens through which we view the world. Consequently, every new experience is filtered through the knowledge of past encounters.

For instance, if one's life has consisted of struggles and denials, that person may easily accept defeat when confronted with obstacles. If a person is accustomed to overcoming obstacles, when faced with a similar circumstance, he/she will be determined to seek an alternative solution. So being trapped is a matter of one's own perception.

Question

Are you willing to change your condition and become the person God created you to be, despite the obstacles?

The Woman

In the story of the woman with the issue of blood, we witness a courageous person who took small steps that proved to be monumental. She had become totally engulfed by her condition. The dreaded twelve-year illness turned into a life of remedy preoccupation, which led up to the moment she met Jesus. In spite of her affliction, she broke through the barriers and captured the healing she desperately needed. ***Her victory was the result of sheer determination, belief in small increments and movement toward a specific goal.***

Problems

Sometimes we define ourselves by past encounters, or by our existing struggles. Problems, left unchecked, have a way of soaking deep into our psyche, and may become a major part of our identity. We begin formulating our self-worth by all of the challenges presented. Before we know it, we are submerged in hopelessness and despair. We find ourselves at a breaking point.

For example, one who has gone through several divorces may accept the term divorcee. A physically challenged person who uses a wheelchair may accept the term handicapped. A person with a manageable disease accepts defeat, and fails to work on lifestyle and diet changes. I conclude that these things are a matter of one's perception that can be addressed by irrational faith. Someone said: "When you are on the bottom, the only way out is up." I firmly believe this saying, and would also add that while we are moving toward our blessing, we should refuse to participate in the acceptance of the problem. In other words, **never accept bad advice about how to navigate through a crisis!** Always assess the status of your condition and the direction that God is leading you. Be determined to find a solution, with the help of the Holy Spirit.

Satan's Agenda

When we are dealing with a difficult problem, one of the enemy's greatest schemes is to make us feel as if we are the only one facing such a pressing issue. The woman, who was sick for twelve years, had become the subject of lies, superstition and homemade remedies. "She had suffered a great deal under the care of many doctors and had spent all she had, yet instead of getting better, she grew worse," (Mk 5:26). Everyone around her saw the problem as uncommon and complicated. Mark refers to her as the woman, which leads some scholars to suggest that she was not known and could have belonged to a neighboring village. Therefore, it may be safe to assume that there were other women in that village with the same illness, but she felt detached.

Just as with this woman, the devil's intent is to convince us that our issues are unsolvable. The ultimate goal is to embed, within our spirit, feelings of isolation, abandonment and hopelessness.

Jesus said: "Simon, Simon, Satan has asked to sift all of you as wheat. But I have prayed for you, Simon, that your faith may not fail. And when you have turned back, strengthen your brothers," (Lk 22:31-32).

<u>God's Agenda</u>

God's purpose is to provide us with spiritual abundance to transcend every obstacle and challenge we face. "The thief comes only to steal and kill and destroy; I have come that they may have life, and have it to the full," (Jn. 10:10). It is important that we not allow anything to take us over the edge; instead, we ought to allow our belief in God's power to take us over the mountain. David said: "Though my father and mother forsake me, the LORD will receive me," (Ps 27:10). In the midst of trouble, it is important to recognize that God is always with us: Regardless of the degree of difficulty, God never leaves. We remain in the everlasting and strong embrace of a God who is forever providing solutions.

Breakthrough

<u>Created</u>

The woman was told that she would never be cured of her disease, but Jesus came along and created within her a genuine and refreshing truth. Christians often say they want a clean heart. This was King David's lament during a period in his life when He felt void of the Holy Spirit, because of his sin with Bathsheba. David asks God: "Create in me a pure heart, O God, and renew a steadfast spirit within me," (Ps 51:10). Webster Dictionary's definition of "create" is to make or produce something; to cause something new to exist; to cause to happen; to bring about and to arrange, as by intention or design.

Irrational faith stands firmly on the belief that real truth is created through the blood of Jesus. "Then you will know the truth, and the truth will set you free," (Jn 8:32). Knowing the truth sets us free from guilt and sin, the only way to know truth is through continued belief in and obedience to God's word. Jesus said: "I am the way, the truth and the life: and no man comes to the Father except through me," (Jn 14:6). Jesus validates real truth in our lives.

On the day of our conversion, we experience a spiritual heart transplant and mind reconstruction. Jesus becomes Lord, and the Holy Spirit emerges as an authentic and permanent resident. "Here I am! I stand at the door and knock. If anyone hears my voice and opens the door, I will come in and eat with that person, and they with me," (Rev. 3:20).

She Thought

She spent everything she had, and now it was time to spend what remained with Jesus. Just as Jesus was passing by, she initiated the first step of a three-step process that would permanently change her condition. Step one was allowing "belief" to enter her mind. Even with the crowd, and a synagogue ruler pleading with Jesus on behalf of his dying daughter, she allowed her mind to be flooded with the belief that she could get close enough to receive the miraculous healing from the cloak of the Master. The widespread imagery of this thought was enough to create a glimmer of hope. ***Thinking about the healing power of Jesus supersedes our dilemma, and creates the space we need to start the engine of transformation.*** This is where we begin to control the problem instead of letting the problem control us. At this juncture, we are envisioning our breakthrough becoming our blessing!

She Spoke

The second step occurred when she spoke victory over her situation. She said to herself: "If I may touch but his clothes, I shall be made whole," (Mk 5:28). Speaking victorious words puts us in the driver's seat, with the key in our hand. This is when we start talking to God about God's plan for our future. " For I know the plans I have for you," declares the LORD, "plans to prosper you and not to harm you, plans to give you hope and a future," (Jer. 29:11). God's ultimate plan is for us to live in victory and peace.

She Moved

She moved in the direction of the blessing. ***Faith, combined with action, immediately changes our status from stagnate to active !*** Taking positive action sets us on the pathway to success. "In the same way, faith by itself, if it is not accompanied by action, is dead," (Jas 2:17). For example, a person who is unemployed must emerge each day with the thought that "This is my day". The thought must be followed by the action of going out in search of a job.

The Blessing

Step three: the blessing is actually a two-part motion, combining the elements of prayer, faith and action. The motions consist of placing the key of prayer in the ignition of faith and turning. The old saints in my church used to say, ***"Baby, prayer is the key and faith unlocks the door."*** Linking the components of prayer and faith with action ignites our mobility, which propels us in the direction of change. ***Irrational faith believes it is fully capable of moving beyond any obstacle.***

> "Therefore, I urge you, brothers and sisters, in view of God's mercy, to offer your bodies as a living sacrifice, holy and pleasing to God—this is your true and proper worship. Do not conform to the pattern of this world, but be transformed by the renewing of your mind. Then you will be able to test and approve what God's will is— His good, pleasing and perfect will," (Rom. 12:1-2).

When we accept Jesus as our Lord and Personal Savior, our minds get renewed by the power of the Holy Spirit. She accepted the belief of wholeness, and visualized herself receiving the miracle.

The Key

Touching His garment brought her instantaneous healing.

> "Immediately, her bleeding stopped and she felt in her body that she was freed from her suffering. At once, Jesus realized that power had gone out from him. He turned around in the crowd and asked, 'Who touched my clothes?'" (Mk 5:29-30).

To his disciples, this seemed like a crazy question, because they were currently being mobbed by so many people. "They said to him, 'Jesus, you see the multitudes upon us, yet you inquire about who touched you?'" (Mk 5:31). To Him, it was no ordinary touch; this was a clinch from someone who had an urgent need.

The woman shrunk down in fear, thinking that He would scold her for being out of place: According to the Jewish laws, she should not have been in a public setting. The law held strict prohibitions for a woman who had this type of illness lasting for a prolonged period of time. (See Lev. 15:25.) His reason for asking the question was not to reveal any wrongdoing, but rather to expose the greater measure of her irrational faith in Him. With quiet hesitation, she faced Jesus and confessed that she was the one who received the cure. He assured her that it was her faith in Him that resulted in her healing. He called her daughter; publically addressing her as daughter established an environment of empowerment. He was essentially commanding her to go forth in a new direction of healing and renewed life.

God called Israel the daughter of Zion: not in reference to an actual person, but as a metaphorical expression of a loving relationship toward them as a nation. (See Zechariah 2:10.) As righteous people of faith, we are all sons and daughters of God. "For those who are led by the Spirit of God are the children of God," (Rom. 8:14).

This was the day that she reached her destination; here is where she snatched her blessing. ***Irrational faith takes us into the realm of breakthrough and blessing.*** It moves with intensity, and makes bold professions.

> "Simon Peter answered, 'Master, we've worked hard all night and haven't caught anything. But because you say so, I will let down the nets.' When they had done so, they caught such a large number of fish that their nets began to break," (Lk 5:5-6).

Life Lesson

<u>Signs</u>

The week of July 19, 1999 was another difficult time in my life. I experienced church conflict, illness of a family member, car trouble and a host of other things that caused me to experience emotional sickness. This is the kind of sickness that is brought on by the stressors of life. I felt stuck, in what one might call a state of limbo, waiting for something to happen. My religious upbringing taught me to never question God, but I had some critical questions. The questions I asked were, when will it happen and when will I move? The "it" was the change I greatly needed. I laughed to keep from crying; I laughed at church, at work, at home with my children and in the presence of extended family members. On the inside I was frustrated, but I still managed to laugh. This laughter was a superficial way for me to mask the disappointment and self-pity I felt about where I was in ministry.

I asked my wife for an honest assessment about what she observed about me emotionally. She told me that I had become anxious. Several of my closest colleagues and parishioners provided me with the same critique, using different words. I could no longer ignore the problem. After making a deeper self-assessment, I discovered that the laughter was something I used to cope in stressful situations.

In my search for an answer, I recalled Dr. Kelly Brown Douglas, my professor at Howard University in the early 1990s, encouraging us to chart our course and consider multiple avenues of ministry. At the time, I rejected her statement: I had made up my mind to go back to my hometown to be a local church pastor and nothing else. I didn't realize it at the time, but her words had settled deep into my subconscious.

On the first Sunday in April, April 2, 2000, I officially resigned from the pastorate and joined the military on May 1, 2000. For the past fourteen years, I have served as a US Army Chaplain. With the exception of marrying my beautiful bride, I can say that this has been one of my greatest life decisions. Leaving my hometown, my church and extended family for a second time was truly a leap of faith. The payoff has been growth in my faith in God and in my own God-given abilities. Through action, persistence and the power of God, I have been able to accomplish many of the things that I had only imagined doing in ministry.

Today, I still believe in signs. God uses signs, not just in earth-shaking events but also in the small voice deep within. Today, I still trust the voice, and I have learned to take action.

New Belief: "Trust in the LORD with all your heart and lean not on your own understanding; in all your ways submit to Him, and He will make your paths straight," (Prov. 3:5-6).

Remember

1- Victory is determination, small increments and movement.

2- Never accept bad advice when you are in a crisis.

3- Real truth is created through the shed blood of Jesus.

4- Jesus supersedes our dilemma and starts transformation.

5- Faith, combined with action, eliminates stagnation.

6- "Prayer is the key and faith unlocks the door."

7- Irrational faith moves beyond any obstacle.

8- Accepting Jesus as Lord renews our mind.

9- Irrational faith takes us into the realm of breakthrough and blessing.

Conclusion

I will be the first to acknowledge that there is no set way of being a promoter of faith. Whether one acts as storyteller or bridge-builder, it does not matter as long as those receiving the message become empowered to grasp a deeper commitment to irrational faith. I see myself as both storyteller and bridge-builder.

It has been said that: "A bridge-builder is one who links areas once separated so that weary travelers may find a refuge on the other side." My goal was to illustrate that irrational faith is essential in the life of every believer. The hope is that the message that the "impossible can be made possible" was conveyed. Progress can be actualized when we stand on the promises in God's holy word. When we fuse the elements of conversion, assurance, prayer , persistence and mobility, we get extraordinary power.

Let us forge ahead with a stronger belief that has been shaped by a spirit of resistance to devastating forces. Someone said, ***"The stuff that doesn't kill you makes you stronger."*** I believe that statement, and would add that there is a bright light at the end of the tunnel of darkness. Most importantly, there lays a blessing on the other side of trouble.

References

Axelrod, J. (2006). The 5 Stages of Loss and Grief. *Psych Central*. Retrieved on March 21, 2014, from http://psychcentral.com/lib/the-5-stages-of-loss-and-grief/000617

Richardson, W.F. (1986). The Power of the Pew: A Call to Partnership. Nashville, TN: Townsend Press.

Thurman, Howard. (1963). Disciplines of the Spirit. New York, NY: Harper and Row.

Milton Keynes UK
Ingram Content Group UK Ltd.
UKHW020727030424
440506UK00002B/463